Feasts and Seasons

Werenfried van Straaten

Aid to the Church in Need

Published by Aid to the Church in Need
124 Carshalton Road
Sutton, Surrey SM1 4RL
Great Britain
Registered Charity No. 265582

© Aid to the Church in Need 1993

Cover design by James Grint

Printed by Caldra House Ltd.
23 Coleridge Street
Hove, Sussex BN3 5AB
Great Britain

ISBN 0951 1805 4 1

INTRODUCTION

Dear Friends,

Abandoned and alone on a cross between heaven and earth, Jesus has ransomed us all. But it is only when we love Him and when we are united to Him that we possess the ransom for our sins and the key to heaven. Our union with Him ought to be more precious to us than all the treasures that the earth can offer us.

But no-one can be united to Him without taking part in His passion and His Cross. That is why the Church is nowhere so flourishing as where she is in need. And she is nowhere so much in danger as where she flees the loneliness of the crucified Christ.

Our Work gives you the possibility of living compassion and thus sharing in the sufferings of Jesus. Beyond all frontiers, we carry something that belongs to you — a piece of your heart, a handful of consolation, a handkerchief to dry their tears   to the countries where the Master is again following His Way of the Cross and where He is dying on the Calvaries of the twentieth century. Through us, you are able to alleviate His Way of the Cross like Veronica or Simon of Cyrene, and to stand at the foot of His Cross like Mary or John. Do not deprive yourself of his possibility. For nothing is more serious than turning away heedlessly from Jesus, who suffers in His Church. And nothing is more precious than consoling the abandoned Jesus, who is present in His persecuted brothers and sisters.

Do not think that it is a question of money: it is a question of love. Your financial sacrifice is worthless if it is made with ulterior motives, if your heart does not bleed for the pain of those who must bleed with the Lamb.

It is by truly suffering with your brothers and sisters in distress, in whom you recognise the Lord, that you can be united with the abandoned Jesus. The consequences of this are beyond counting: in Him you possess God, in whom you find not only heaven, with the Holy Trinity, but also the earth, with the whole of humanity. In Him you possess all things, for you make your own all that is His.

This high vocation is dearly bought. For Christ, on the Cross, lost His awareness of the presence of God. All that was left to Him was suffering without escape, total failure, the loneliness of one who feels himself abandoned by God and man. That suffering — the price of the Redemption — becomes yours too, if you truly love the abandoned Christ and are united to Him.

We are not always ready for this calling. As long as we remain rebellious and embittered by an injustice undergone, our suffering is not His. As long as we defend ourseves desperately against humiliation, slander, or the destruction of everything we have built up for God, we are not united to the Crucified. As long as we seek all-too-human ways out in order to avoid the worst, we do not have the spirit of Christ. Our suffering remains barren, and our loss will be in vain.

The basic law of Christiani is that we should die like the grain of wheat that falls to the ground, if we want to bear fruit or eternity. That is why, for us too, the honour of Calvary will strike, in a long illness, perhaps, or when death tears from us the one we love most, in our great grief for a lost child, in injustice or failure, in the loneliness of old age, in the poverty or great persecution which is at our doors. We do not know the hour of our Calvary; we know only that God does not try anyone beyond their strength.

Let us cling, then, to the image of the Man of Sorrows who is crucified in millions of Christians. Do not let yourself be taken up with the little worries of each day, to the point where your forget the day when you must accept your last cross. Fight against your human respect, against cowardice, fear of suffering, against your passions and your sins. Practice accepting the little crosses that God sends to you. Deny yourself something — a real privation for you, and a consolation for others — in order to lighten the Cross under which those chosen by Jesus are bowed down. And beg God to give to all who carry the Cros alone the strength to share in the lot of the abandoned Jesus. Pray for the Church in need, pray for yourselves, and pray too for your

Werenfried — Straat

FIRST WEEK OF ADVENT

God has gone

At the beginning of Advent, Holy Church in her liturgy asks us to apply to ourselves the terrible reproaches that God once made to His people by the Prophet Isaiah. The Church considers it necessary that the mightiest preacher in the history of religion, who proclaimed and prepared the Kingdom of God in the eighth century before Christ, should cry out to God's people today: 'A sinful nation, a people weighed down with guilt, a breed of wrong-doers, perverted sons. They have abandoned God, despised the Holy One of Israel, they have turned away from Him.'[1]

We must admit that we have abandoned God. That we live without God. That God is gone. For if He were with us the world would look different. God is present in creation by His law, in which the meaning of life is anchored. Trees, flowers, sun, wind and all other things, animals too, fulfil this law from inner necessity. If there were not man, the vast body of the world would breathe peacefully and grow harmoniously because it would be animated by God, whose law would be fulfilled without hindrance.

But there is man with his freedom. With the possibility of deciding for or against God. With the power to say no. When God commands he may rebel and answer: 'No, God, I don't have to do that and You can't ask it of me. Order someone else. I won't do it!' And the unfathomable God does not crush this man to nothing but allows His law to be pushed aside. And as He is one with His law He allows Himself to be pushed aside too. So man can reject God. He becomes the leaking hole in creation. Through him

[1] Is 1:4

God's life and animating spirit flow out of the world. So man becomes the door through which God leaves the world.

God has gone. But every man is also the door through which He wants to return. Once He came back through the sacred Humanity of Jesus Christ. But now He seeks access to this world in the millions of new humanity. Christmas is drawing near. His day is at hand. He comes back into the world, if we give Him room in our hearts. If we accept Him in His law of love. If we fulfil Mary's task: to conceive Jesus and bear Him within us so that He becomes the heart of our own life. Then He will love the Heavenly Father with all our heart, with all our soul, and with all our strength. Then His love, His goodness, His pity for men will shine out through our eyes, help with our hands, and live anew in us His redeeming life of long ago. Then we shall be the doors, the thousands, the hundreds of thousands, the millions of doors, the gates opening wide through which He, the Lord, the Prince of Peace, God-with-us, will come into His world, into His kingdom.

Yes, come Lord Jesus, come to set us free, show us Your face and we shall be saved. O Emmanuel, our King and Lawgiver, the Awaited and Saviour of the nations, come to our aid, O Lord our God!

SECOND WEEK OF ADVENT

The Star of Bethlehem

When you look into the night sky in these weeks before Christmas, think of the star that at God's command appeared in the heavens at the right moment to show the three kings the way to the Divine Infant, and think of the angels who hastened to Bethlehem to announce the birth of the Saviour to the shepherds. God was generous with miracles when carrying out His plan of salvation. It is therefore no fault of God's if there is no peace on earth or in our hearts. It is the fault of all those who are not of good will. It is the fault of you and me whenever, blind to God's star and deaf to the angels' song, we selfishly go our own way, away from the crib.

No hurt can touch us if at the crib we are ready to learn the first steps towards this true life: to become small like a child, to arm ourselves with the faith of the three wise men and to clothe ourselves with the humility of the shepherds. In return we receive God's immeasurable gifts of love, peace and eternal life. I wish you these with all my heart.

THIRD WEEK OF ADVENT

The Tragedy of the Christmas story

Soon it will be Christmas. The glittering Christmas tree and the old carols ringing out around the crib or on the radio will remind you of the unforgettable story of Mary and Joseph, journeying because of an Emperor's whim through the difficult mountain country to Bethlehem, where there was no room for them at the inn. Thus began the story of our own salvation.

Our salvation was dearly bought, not only on Calvary but also in Bethlehem. The song of the angels, the goodness of the shepherds and the faith of the wise men should never cause us to forget the tragedy that comes down to us in the Christmas story. The tragedy of closed doors and hearts. The scandal of loveless inhospitality and of the stable in which the Lord was born. The hatred of Herod, who saw a political danger in the defenceless baby. The fear of Mary and Joseph, forced to flee suddenly, head over heels into the street, to the frontier late in the night, fleeing breathlessly from one hiding place to another, while behind them the shrieks of the dying children and the despairing screams of their mothers rose to heaven. It is easy to imagine the rest: the arrival in Egypt, the toilsome start in a strange land, the language difficulties, the interview with the police, the mistrust, the tramp from official to official, the formalities to obtain permits for residence and work.... Who feels like giving work to a foreigner who came over the frontier illegally with wife and child?

Jesus, Mary and Joseph were the first refugees of the Christian era. Countless others were to share their fate later on. Since the night when the angel woke Joseph and told him to flee to Egypt with the child and His mother, the world has been full of the hunted, the persecuted, and the refugees in whom Christ begs for love and help. And just as once the shepherds brought the Christ Child cheese or milk or a warm sheepskin, and just as there were kind-hearted people here and there on the way to Egypt who took pity on the Holy Family, so it is now our task to help the persecuted Christ of today wherever He is suffering need in the least of His brothers.

Christmas is more than a family festival with a Christmas tree, candle-light, tinsel, and turkey on the table. It is Christ's coming into a cold, dark, unredeemed world. Certainly at Christmas you may celebrate the incarnation of God with all the joy of redeemed man. There can be no objection to preparing a festive meal. But you must not forget what is essential: that Christ wants to become man again in His holy Church and in each one of us, so that in us His form, His goodness, His mercy, His love for men and His helpfulness may shine out in the darkness of this age.

FOURTH WEEK OF ADVENT

The peace of Christ

I will ask the Child in the manger to send you, notwithstanding weakness, uncertainty and fear, that peace which the angels on Christmas night promised to all men of good will.[2]

This peace will be yours to the extent that you allow Christ to become the head and heart of your life. More than ever, you must take your bearings from Him who is the eternal truth. The thoughts and works of the Son of God made man must be the only pattern for your lives. Each of His words and each of His deeds recounted in the Gospel must be more precious to you than all human wisdom and more valuable than all new doctrines.

There is no need to fear that weakness and sin may separate you from Him, as long as you humbly acknowledge that human nature has been wounded by Original Sin. Do not be afraid if you are sometimes unable to distinguish what is right from what is mistaken, disobedience from inspiration, the chaff from the wheat. You need not be ashamed, for our Saviour Himself said that false Christs and false prophets would arise who, if possible, would deceive even the chosen.[3] I advise you therefore to listen to the words of the Pope.

It is not without good grounds that the Church begins her Christmas liturgy with a description of the battle between the Messiah and the Powers of Darkness. Herod is still trying to kill the Child by murdering unborn life. Satan is doing his utmost to separate believers from Christ. He finds his helpers, who darken the Lord's splendour and debase Him.

[2] Lk 2:14
[3] Mt 24:24

We do not know how many more Christmases will be given us as a source of grace to cleanse us from sin and wickedness. So when the Lord comes, let us love Him so fervently that He will want to stay with us. Let us realise that all power proceeds from Him alone. Let us, who are weak, kneel daily in a spirit of penitence before the tabernacle, that God's anger may be averted from His people; that the good may become holier, the lukewarm more ardent, the rich poorer and all of us more humble; that those gone astray may find their way back to the truth, and that our own hearts may be cleansed. Only in this way can Christ, lying so helpless in the manger, grow in us and fill us with His love.

CHRISTMAS EVE

'Tomorrow injustice will be swept away from the earth!'

Those who follow the liturgy of Advent and await the Redeemer cannot keep Christmas as a sentimental, romantic festival. It is for them the royal festival of the Mighty God who has meted out time and in the fullness of time will come to deliver His people from injustice and slavery. Although momentarily He has hidden Himself in the shape of a harmless child, Herod sees in Him the great Adversary against whom he mobilises his army. Therefore the Church begins its Office of the Nativity with the grand description of the conflict between the Messiah and the Powers of Darkness. It describes how God empties the vials of His wrath upon the raging heathens and upon the rebellious kings of the earth; how He appoints His Christ and gives Him the nations as a heritage, to govern them with an iron sceptre.... This strong Christ, to whom all power is given in heaven and earth,[4] is the Redeemer awaited with fervent longing by the oppressed. Emphatically, therefore, the Church proclaims the encouraging news on the Eve of Christmas: 'Tomorrow injustice will be swept away from the earth!'

This does not mean that we — like the Jews — are to expect a political Messiah, or that we may imagine the redemption as a punitive expedition against exploiters and dictators, or as a social reformation to change the world into a paradise. Christ is not a politician, nor a general, nor a trade-union leader. He is the Son of God, who was made man in order to grant God's life to the world, and who demands on these grounds that we be perfect even as our heavenly Father is

---

[4] Mt 28:19

perfect.[5] Only to the extent that we comply with this demand shall injustice be swept from the earth.

We are personally responsible for the piece of God's kingdom that we are ourselves. Only when Christ is the only standard of our actions... only then is Christ present in these times and is born in us, and there can be peace on earth around us. But should there be no room in the inn of our hearts for Christ, after Christmas the injustice will be just as great as ever before.

---

[5] Mt 5:48

CHRISTMAS DAY

It is Christmas a thousand times a year

At the time of the first Christmas day the roads leading to Bethlehem were crowded with people hurrying to the City of David to have themselves written down in the census. They worked with hands, feet and elbows to get ahead of the crowd, knowing well that only the first few people would have a chance to find lodgings for the night. And as so often happens, the rich and the powerful, those riding on horseback or on camels or in heavy coaches pushed ahead of the lesser people on their donkeys and snapped up all the available rooms in the inns, so that for Mary, who was carrying Jesus, there was no place in the inn. She knew that her time had come. Joseph was at his wits' end, but there was no help for it. Lonely and forgotten, they wandered forlornly among the crowds....

Nothing much has changed. There will never be room for Christ as long as people think too much of themselves. There is nothing wrong with our being well off. We may be pleased with a house or the cosiness of a room with glass in the windows to keep out the cold. We may be glad that we have all we want, but do we remember that Mary and Joseph in their thousands are wandering outside throughout the world, and that they are carrying Christ who is crying in all the refugees and outcasts, in all He has called the least of His children and beneath whose misery He has concealed the glory of His form?

It is Christmas a thousand times a year and a thousand times Jesus is asking to be received. But a thousand times a year the story repeats itself of the predatory crowd in Bethlehem, of the heedless inn-keepers and well-fed citizens in their self-sufficiency. And a thousand times doors and hearts are closed against the bitterness of distress which is Christ's distress.

CHRISTMAS DAY

Christmas without Christ?

Will the Divine Child be missing this Christmas night? Will the cribs remain empty? Will Jesus in fact permit Himself to be born anew in this murderous age? That depends on us. We must be the doors through which He comes into the world again. We must fulfil Mary's role: to conceive Him spiritually and bear Him in our hearts, so that He becomes the heart of our lives and the sole guideline of our actions. For only if we do what He did and reject what He rejected, only when His burning love for God and for man shines through us into the world, only when shepherds and kings, the powerful and the oppressed sink to their knees because they discern in today's People of God the living presence of the Redeemer: only then will Christ be born anew in this age.

So let us this Christmas once more be what our Heavenly Father called us into life to be: the image of the Beloved Son, in whom is all His delight.[6] Let us belong to the one hundred and forty-four thousand who follow the Lamb.[7] The sign on our forehead must be love.

---

[6] Is 42:1
[7] Rev 14:1-4

THE FLIGHT INTO EGYPT

One particular case

May I ask your special attention for one particular case? It regards a homeless husband and wife with a newborn child who, owing to a régime of terror exercised by a dictator, have had to flee to a foreign country. The husband is unemployed. The wife is homesick in the strange country, where refugees are not welcome. The child is hungry and its name is Jesus.

Jesus, Mary and Joseph were the first persecuted people of the Christian era, the forerunners of the multitudes who up to the present day have had to share their fate. In each of these Christ is present according to His Word: 'Whatsoever you do to the least of My children you do to Me.'[8] He is therefore not separated from you by two thousand years. He is your contemporary.

---

[8] Mt 25:45

NEW YEAR

New Year's wishes

The new year that God gives us is an empty space that we must fill in ourselves. What matters most is not what it will bring us, but what we make of it. It is like the frame of a picture on which we must work for a whole year. A picture — best if painted in bright, cheerful colours — but in which the dark shadows are also necessary because there can be no picture without shadows.

It is a bad habit to say nothing but pleasant things in our New Year's greetings. A year filled exclusively with money, pleasure and enjoyment is a failure. Although I hope that joy, peace and happiness may be yours in abundance, I know that you will not be spared hard things too. Therefore I wish you the strength to take upon yourselves everything that is needed in order to make your life a spectacle with which God will be satisfied.[9] And as God's plan for you all is to become like the image of His Son, your life should be a re-enactment of the life of Christ.[10]

---

[9] 1 Cor 4:9
[10] Col 2:6

NEW YEAR

A year has started

A year has ended and a year has begun — a year of world history and a year of little events that happen to us personally. A brief moment between two eternities.

A year is not much. But God gives it to us to make something beautiful out of it. And therefore it *is* a lot. Let us use it in order to give joy to our Lord Jesus Christ, who lives in our midst in the least of His brothers.

Scripture says that Christ came to bring fire to the earth.[11] That was two thousand years ago; but He returns again and again with the golden spark of His love. He lays it in our hearts to make them warm and generous and glowing with divine love. With this fire, in the year God has granted us, we must make it light and warm for all those who live in cold and darkness. For it is the joy of the All-Highest to see the fire of Christ burning. So my first wish is that you should carry the fire of God's love through the world for another whole year.

---

[11] Lk 12:49

JANUARY

Renewing our lives

Do not be afraid! Our salvation is in our own hands. For the Prince of Darkness is not to be feared because he opposes God, but because we forget God; not because he is strong in hate, but because we are weak in love; not because he kills Christians, but because we do not live as Christians and are shackled to this earth with a thousand chains. We do not persecute Christ, but we compromise Him. As long as we detract from Christ's splendour with our materialism and selfishness, we shall not have the strength to draw all the searching people of our times to Him[12] who so fervently desires to rule in their hearts too.

In this new year may God grant you and me the grace to recognise this and to renew our lives accordingly.

---

[12] Jn 12:32

FEBRUARY

The hidden life of Jesus

The Christmas season is over. To the song of the angels Christ was born. Shepherds and kings adored Him. Herod tried to kill Him. He fled to Egypt and returned to Nazareth. There His hidden life began.

The hidden life was not a waste of time. The thirty years in which He 'increased in wisdom, in stature, and in favour with God and men'[13] were no less important than the time of His public ministry. God's favour rested on His beloved Son, as was made known at His baptism in the Jordan by 'a voice from heaven';[14] it preceded all the words and miracles with which Jesus astonished the world. Many years before the Father transfigured His only-begotten Son on Mount Tabor, the hidden life of Jesus in Nazareth found His favour.

For love of His Father our Lord wants to live on in the Church, too. From day to day the Holy Spirit showers on the Church all the graces she needs to make manifest the life of Jesus in all its aspects. For in all ages the Church must show 'Christ in all His fullness'.[15] So the Church must not only continue the amazing work with which our Lord concluded His life on earth; she must also imitate all that He did for thirty years in His hidden life as the carpenter's son.

---

[13] Lk 2:40
[14] Lk 3:22
[15] Eph 4:13

FEBRUARY

Blessed are the pure in heart

What consolation can I give you? The consolation of the Faith against which the gates of Hell cannot prevail.[16] And the comfort of Jesus' word that those who first of all seek God's Kingdom and His righteousness will receive all the rest.[17] Including the strength to live in purity: birth control according to God's plan, the answer to the population explosion, the solution to the problems of our society. Hence it follows that Jesus' message of the Kingdom of God is being falsely interpreted by those who no longer ask of the Church the strength to control their instincts but a licence to live their lives to the full with a clear conscience. The constitution of God's Kingdom cannot be altered by the democratic majority decision of a 'pluralistic' society. For this reason it remains true that we do not live for ourselves but must yield ourselves to God with all our hearts, with all our souls, and with all our strength.[18]

Only the pure in heart can see God[19] and only he who loves the truth can hear God's voice. This ancient rule is still valid. The more clearly the structural lines are arranged in a crystal, the purer is the light that shines through it. And the more impure the soul and spirit of a man, the less clearly does he observe the divine light and the less visible does God become to him in the world. Impurity makes a man just as blind to God's reality as to the reality of the devil. That is why an impure person, in spite of his intelligence, loses the ability to 'discern spirits'.

Let us turn now full of trust to God. If we listen to Him, He will speak; and if we obey Him, He will act. And if God acts, miracles will happen.

---

[16] Mt 16:18
[17] Mt 6:33
[18] Deut 6:5; Lk 10:27
[19] Mt 5:8

MARCH

The cycle of the seasons

Year in, year out, winter and spring, summer and autumn follow one another as the seasons pass. We se nature die only to be born again, green and springlike. We have seen it so often that dead leaves, bare trees and empty fields no longer cause us concern. We know that if the grain of wheat does not fall in the ground and die, it remains alone; but if it dies it bears much fruit.

With the Romans the year began in March. For them the newborn spring was the beginning, the barren winter the end. In the Christian calendar we celebrate the new year when nature is dead. It is not really dead, however, but sleeping — like Jairus' daughter.[20] God takes her by the hand. Less touching but just as full of hope is the drama of Good Friday, when Christ bled to death on His cross to rise again on Easter morning.

---

[20] Mk 5:39

MARCH

We are the salt of the earth

We have a great responsibility on our shoulders. We have the Gospel, the Sacraments and the warning voice of ecclesiastical authority. Through our centuries-long traditions we know better than others the difference between good and evil. More than others we are obliged to lead spotless lives, to practise charity, prayer and apostolic zeal. For it may depend on us whether Christ's name shall be blessed or cursed by people and nations who can only know Him through our example. The saying 'You are the salt of the earth'[21] applies to us all. If the salt has lost its savour, it will be cast away: this has often happened, and can also happen to us.

---
[21] Mt 5:13

ASH WEDNESDAY

We must not think that we are without guilt

'Remember, man, that you are dust, and to dust you shall return.'[22] These words of Ash Wednesday remind us not only of the sentence pronounced in Paradise but also of the sinfulness that led to it. We must not think that we are without guilt. We all share the guilt for the suffering in this world. We must let our forty days of Lent be marked by our desire to make reparation for the evil we have done. I believe that all of us must live more spiritually and in penance, and not lose sight of humble prayer and old-fashioned mortification, besides love. For love, prayer and penance are the indispensible corner-stones of God's Kingdom on earth.

---

[22] Mass of Ash Wednesday, verse for imposition of ashes; cf. Gen 2:7

FIRST WEEK IN LENT

Turn again to the Lord your God

After the feast-days of the Christmas cycle, the time of fasting and penance has begun. A long time has passed since God by His incarnation came down into His creation. The Church has celebrated this joyful event, but war, famine, injustice, terror, blood and tears have spoilt the festive mood. And the miracle of the Word that was made flesh in order to dwell among us has become unworthy of belief for countless people who are waiting in vain for the radical transformation that the return of God into the world should bring about.

The Prophet Isaiah has described the signs that must accompany this transformation: 'The wilderness and the dry lands will exult and the wasteland rejoice and blossom and bring forth flowers like the crocus. Then the eyes of the blind shall be opened and the ears of the deaf unsealed, then the lame shall leap like a deer and the tongues of the dumb sing for joy.'[23] The peoples will hammer their swords into ploughshares and their spears into pruning knives. Nation will not lift sword against nation, there will be no more training for war.'[24]

The absence of these signs of salvation must lead us to fear that God, who has come to His own people, has once again not been accepted by them. If it is true that God came to us in order to bring the world life, peace and happiness, then when God is banished from His creation it must have unforeseeable consequences and bring about catastrophes....

---

[23] Is 35:1-2, 5-6
[24] Is 2:4

25

I asked myself what we must do in this situation. I read the answer in the Holy Scriptures: 'Thus says the Lord: come back to Me with all your heart, with fasting and weeping. Rend your hearts and not your garments and turn again to the Lord your God. Keep a holy fast. Call the people together. Let the people keep watch in prayer. Between the forecourt and the altar let the priests lament and cry: Spare your people, Lord, and do not let your heritage be put to shame.'[25] Years ago I proposed to you to return to the tradition of a fast linked with prayer and good works. Now I repeat the appeal. May God strengthen in you the spirit of penance.

Most of us live a life which is stained with unfaithfulness. We are all — laity, priests and bishops — a Church of poor sinners. All too often we deny the Cross that from age to age must redeem the world. That is why in this season of Lent the call to conversion is addressed to each one of us.

---

[25] Joel 2:12-13, 15-17

SECOND WEEK IN LENT

Man does not live on bread alone

The Son of God became man in order to re-establish His Father's kingdom on earth. Before He began His public life, He withdrew into the wilderness to pray and fast. Having fasted for forty days and forty nights He was hungry. Then the Tempter came to Him and said: 'If you are the Son of God, command these stones to become bread.'[26]

Everyone who feels called to renew the face of the earth and to lead his contemporaries to a brighter future lays himself open to this temptation: 'Turn these stones into bread for the poor; stay their hunger without their having to lift a finger; promise everybody a life of abundance, free from all cares; establish a paradise in which there are neither rich nor poor; rule with ease over a people whose stomachs are full — what more could they ask for!' But Jesus answered: 'Man cannot live on bread alone but on every word that comes from the mouth of God.'[27]

After the Fall, Adam was told: 'In the sweat of your face you shall eat bread.'[28] But because man cannot live on bread alone, his earthly happiness does not depend solely on a well-ordered economy, which cannot function without 'sweat'. His happiness depends above all on whether rulers and subjects, oppressors and oppressed, rich and poor are prepared to open their eyes and their hearts to every word that comes from the mouth of God.

The Church must make Christ visible in today's world, proclaim His Gospel and help the People of God to imitate

---

[26] Mt 4:2-3
[27] Mt 4:4; Deut 8:3
[28] Gen 3:19

Him. For only if the heavenly Father recognises His child — the Lamb of God who takes away the sins of the world and the Man of Sorrows who redeems through His passion and Cross — in the millions of those baptised in this generation, only then can today's world hope for mercy, forgiveness and salvation.

THIRD WEEK IN LENT

The Church's task to relieve human need

Perhaps God, who is a God of patience, is waiting for us to act. Perhaps He is prepared to accept the bad will or blindness of the great people of this earth because they are not the ones He has destined to solve the problem of hunger and disease. Perhaps He has reserved this task for His Church, which has been commanded to preach the love of the Lord and to demonstrate it. That is part of its message. Just as Christ Himself went around doing good, feeding the hungry and healing the sick, so the Church should relieve human need. Its preaching of salvation would not be credible and would become purely academic if it did not stress its gospel of love by practical help. And if God really intends to restore everything and once more combine and reunite everything under the one Head who is Christ, how greatly would not this grand plan be served if we, in Christ's name, were to solve the world problem of hunger. Why should we not achieve it ourselves? Why cannot Christianity become so ready to make sacrifices that the Church would really be able to give examples and to show models for the solution of this problem?

FOURTH WEEK IN LENT

Rich or poor for eternity?

Why are we so much better off than the countless people in whom the Master is suffering and dying? Why need not *your* child starve to death? Why are *you* not deprived of your means of livelihood if you attend Mass on Sunday? Why do *you* not live separated from all you love? I do not know, and neither do you. It is a mystery. We are no better than the others, and yet we are better off: we, the small minority living in peace and prosperity, have quite a different way to heaven than the vast majority perishing in distress and terror, in pain and hunger. But I think that all these afflicted people will be rich in eternity because they are the least of His little ones, and therefore God's most beloved children. After a short time of deep sorrow, God Himself will dry their eyes,[29] because they will have become identified with the Man of Sorrows.

But *we* shall be poor in eternity for having such a tiny piece of Jesus' cross to bear. That is why God will test us in our brotherly love. If we do not go to our brothers and sisters who are now being crucified for our sins, with hands full of goodness and comfort, if we are miserly with our plenty, if we do not give all we can spare to the poor and persecuted, if we do not become much more heroic in our love, then we should tremble for our eternal salvation.

Lent is no longer the strict fast it was. But it cannot be God's intention that we should not abstain from something in this time of recollection and penance. Can we not bend with greater love over the distress of others who are also suffering for our sakes? That love ought to cost us something.

---

[29] Is 25:8; Rev 21:4

Nowhere can we find in the Gospel that we must practise charity in such a way that our standard of life will not suffer. There is no reason why it should not make us poorer. Let us beseech God to grant us the strength, for the sake of the comfort we must bring to our persecuted brothers, to be satisfied with a cheaper car, or no car at all, less exclusive clothes, a holiday nearer home, a shorter journey, to smoke or drink less, with simpler meals, cheaper toys for the children. For only the love that makes us poorer can make us rich.

FIFTH WEEK IN LENT

We can judge only ourselves

Jesus hides Himself by preference in poor and weak people, whom He has called 'the least of My little ones'.[30] If we consider it our task to console Him and help Him there where He is weeping because He is again being hated, persecuted, imprisoned, tortured and crucified, we already know beforehand that Jesus is now no longer suffering and dying in the unrepeatable and inimitable perfection of His own sacred Humanity, but in the faulty humanity of those who though incorporated in Him by baptism yet live sinful lives.

The Church on earth is not only the Communion of Saints but equally the Church of sinners. All human suffering — except that of Christ — will therefore be burdened with some measure of guilt. And it will never be difficult to show that a religious persecution was directed against a Church consisting of imperfect Popes, bishops, priests and faithful. But it is nowhere written in the Gospel that we must increase the suffering of the afflicted by covering them with reproaches. Nowhere is it written that we are obliged to judge our brothers. If there is any question of blame, then never in respect of others whom we cannot and may not judge, but only of our own guilt and responsibility.

---

[30] Mt 25:45

PASSIONTIDE

We must glory in the Cross of Christ

In this Passiontide, in which we remember the suffering, death, and resurrection of our Lord Jesus Christ, no trial must make us lose courage. More than ever we must glory in the Cross, in which is our salvation, our life and our resurrection. The Cross is not a curse but a blessing and is inseparable from Christianity. Each of us must relive on earth the life of Christ. Therefore our task not only consists in preaching His gospel and practising His love, but above all in sharing personally His sacrifice on the Cross, which He continues to offer until the end of time.

Although the Cross is foolishness and a stumbling-block[34] to the unbelieving generation whose voice is often raised so loud in the Church today, for countless numbers of the faithful — the sick, the lonely, the misunderstood, the aged, those who fear for the Church, the oppressed and the persecuted — it is still the height of wisdom, and they are unwavering in their loyalty to it. It is thanks to them that our Heavenly Father can still see His beloved Son in the spiritual wilderness of today and refrains from cursing His faithless people forever.

We cannot and may not remove the Cross from a world that is yearning for redemption; there is therefore nothing else for us to do but to help our Lord, who suffers in His afflicted brethren, to carry His Cross. It is the age-old task of Veronica and Simon of Cyrene, a task that is everywhere more pressing than ever. While Judas is honoured, the Lord, forsaken by all, is dragged to the place of His execution. Tired to exhaustion, He collapses under spiritual and

---
[34] 1 Cor 1:23

physical pressure. This is not a man staggering along, this is a worm crawling up Calvary. Once more he is suspended between heaven and earth: 'I thirst',[35] He says, and 'My God, why have You forsaken me?'[36]

If we really love this forsaken Christ, who is crucified anew, we may not deny the Cross in our lives. For no one can be united to Him unless they share in His sufferings. This is why the Church is nowhere so flourishing as where it suffers persecution, and nowhere so deep in need as where it shuns the Cross.

---

[35] Jn 19:28; Ps 22:15
[36] Ps 22:1

HOLY WEEK

A 'sensible' Messiah?

Christ entered upon His Passion with the clear conviction: 'Amen, I say to you: one of you will betray me.'[31] And He added: 'It were better for that man if he had never been born.'[32] 'That man' was the one who had been offended when Mary Magdalen had anointed Jesus' feet: 'Why was this ointment not sold for two hundred pence, and given to the poor?'[33]

Judas' question seems very Christian and modern. And yet it is the question of the traitor who neither understands the Lord nor loves the poor, however charitable he may pretend to be. For in his criticism of Mary's gesture of immeasurable love he sets himself apart from the Master's way of thinking, which is to offer Himself up for love unto the foolishness of the Cross. Judas could accept a 'sensible' Messiah, a miracle-worker or a king, but not one who was crucified. For this reason he betrayed Him with the typical argument of one who has known Christ. For only such a person can reject the Cross of Christ under cover of Christian words. Thus Judas has become the father of all those who, for the sake of their own imaginary wisdom, can no longer bear the foolishness of the Cross and therefore argue it away in the name of a 'pure', 'modern' and 'credible' Christianity.

---

[31] Jn 13:21
[32] Mk 14:21
[33] Jn 12:5

MAUNDY THURSDAY

Christ's priests

We call the Church the Mystical Body of Christ. This means among other things that through the centuries Christ must continue to suffer in His Church what He once suffered in His life on earth. Persecuted by Herod, hated by the Pharisees, betrayed by Judas, forsaken by His disciples, He died like a criminal on the Cross. In the history of the Church these phases of His life are repeated over and over again. Today in His Mystical Body He is living in the hour of Gethsemane, when Judas handed Him over and the other apostles abandoned Him, only an hour or two after they had been ordained priests. Eleven of them came back. Which of us was always so true that he never needed to come back?

We priests are the greatest risk in the spreading of the Kingdom of God. Christ took on this risk, although He knew each of us whom He intended to call. Therefore He will reward all who help lessen this risk by accompanying a priest with their prayers and sacrifices.

Never must we priests forget that Christ, who is the light of the world,[37] sends us into the world to shine out as a light[38] in spite of our weakness and to be recognisable as Christ living on in the world. He does not send us to adapt to the world but to follow Him. That binds us by duty to a life of faith and trust in our heavenly Father, a life of prayer, humility, self-denial and love of the Cross, a life in which we accept the Word of God with a pure heart and faithfully preach it.

---

[37] Jn 1:9
[38] Cf. Mt 5:16

GOOD FRIDAY

Forsaken Jesus

Jesus, forsaken and alone on a cross between heaven and earth, has redeemed us all. Only if we love Him and are united with Him do we possess the ransom for our sins and the key to the Kingdom of Heaven. Our unity with Him should therefore be more precious to us than all the treasures on earth.

No one can be united with the Lord without sharing in His suffering and Cross. So that the Church is nowhere so flourishing as where she is suffering persecution or is in need for Christ's sake. And she is nowhere so in need as where she flees from the forsakenness of the Crucified.

Only if in your heart you truly share the sorrow of your brethren in need, in whom you recognise the Lord, can you be united with the forsaken Jesus. The consequences are unimaginable. In Him you possess God, in whom you find not only heaven with the Blessed Trinity, but also the earth with the whole of humanity. In Him you possess everything, for everything that is His will be yours too.[39]

To be chosen like this will cost you dear. For in the crucified Lord the consciousness of God's presence was gone. All He had left was hopeless pain, total failure and the loneliness of those who feel forsaken by God and man. This sorrow, too, which is the price of redemption, will be yours if you truly love Jesus forsaken and are united with Him.

It is the basic law of Christianity that, like the grain of wheat,[40] we must die in the earth in order to bear fruit for

---
[39] 1 Cor 3:22
[40] Jn 12:24

eternity. Therefore one day we too shall come to our Calvaries. Perhaps in a lingering illness or when death takes from us those whom we love most. Perhaps in our grief for a child who has gone astray, or in injustice or failure, in the loneliness of old age, in poverty or in the terrible persecution of the Faith. We do not know when the hour of our Calvary will come. We know only that God does not let anyone be tested beyond his strength.

So keep your gaze fixed on the Man of Sorrows. Do not let the little everyday troubles so occupy your mind that you forget the day on which you must take on your shoulders your last and heaviest cross. Fight against your anxiety about what others may think, against your cowardice and fear of suffering, against your passions and sins. Exercise yourselves in bearing the little crosses that God entrusts to you.

HOLY SATURDAY

Pietá

The picture portrays the Mother of Sorrows with her dead Son in her arms. The body of Jesus is marked by His terrible death agonies. His head rests on Mary's knee. His right hand is cramped from the pain of the piercing. The index finger of the left hand points downwards: 'There, among men, is the cause of My suffering.' The last tears still glimmer in the closing eyes. The gaping wound on the left shoulder comes from the heavy Cross He carried. From this wound our eye is led to the Mother's heart which, pierced with swords,[41] has suffered everything with Jesus in burning love. Can this Mother turn her eyes away from her dead Son? Yes, she can! She looks up to heaven, to the Father, to whom she now again, trustingly, gives her assent, as once at Nazareth.

A breath of peace enfolds this picture of sorrow and tears. It is the peace that Jesus has promised to all who are persecuted, reviled and calumnied for His sake. It is the peace of the martyrs. To the Mother of Sorrows we pray with our beloved Pope: 'O Immaculate Virgin, we will be wholly yours and walk with you the way of unreserved loyalty to Christ and His Church!'

---

[41] Lk 2:35

THE EASTER VIGIL

Alleluia!

Christ is risen indeed.[42] This is the day that the Lord has made: let us rejoice and be glad in it.[43] Alleluia, alleluia, alleluia!

The Easter alleluia explodes after the long lenten fast like an unconquerable victory cry of the risen Christ. But in spite of two thousand Feasts of the Resurrection and millions of alleluias, the world has changed little. Life continues its usual course: crime, corruption, cowardice, fraud, treachery, murder, war, hate, hate and hate again. The hate of men, nations and systems that are never tired of destroying.

Is there a gaping chasm between the alleluias and reality? Is the Easter alleluia a meaningless, empty cry? No! The Church Militant, to which we all belong, stands in the midst of the reality of warring mankind. The alleluia is hers through faith in the Cross and Resurrection. It is the victory chant of the Christ who died and, against all the laws of nature, rose again, who makes our atonement with God and gives us His own life, so that with Him we may defy this terrible epoch.

---

[42] Lk 24:34
[43] Ps 117:24

EASTER DAY

'Why do you seek the living among the dead?'

If ever a thing was hopeless, it was the cause that Christ stood for. It was hopeless on Good Friday, when He died on the Cross and was buried under a heavy stone. Everything was finished. His enemies returned to routine business. But it was not finished. It was the real beginning. Many times this has been repeated in history. The Church was often in a hopeless situation. Its epitaph was already prepared. But each time there came a new beginning. That is the certainty of those who believe in almighty God and in Him whom He has sent: Jesus Christ, our Lord.

We must seek the risen Christ as the women did who came to the sepulchre on Easter morning. To us too the angel says: 'Why do you seek the living among the dead?'[44] No, do not seek life among the dead, among those who have no love and lie buried in the grave of their selfishness. Man can only live by love. And all the injustice on earth, all the misery, all the fear and terror, all the persecution and oppression, all the wars and bloodbaths are only possible through lack of love. For whatever inhuman plans the tyrants and dictators of our age may contrive, the cause is always to be found with the dead. Why do you seek the living among the dead? Among those who live only for themselves, for their money, their possessions and their enjoyment?

So let the risen Christ reign in you, so that through His transforming power you may be renewed. Do not seek life among the dead, among the egoists. Act according to the words of Jesus: 'I give you a new commandment, that you

---
[44] Lk 24:5

should love one another.'[45] Then you, like Peter, John, the holy women, the disciples of Emmaus, will be renewed. They were afraid no more, they bore witness, they had love.

Only if you have love can Christ meet you too and say: 'Peace be with you!'[46] Where there is no love, peace is impossible. There is no way out but love.

---

[45] Jn 13:34
[46] Lk 24:36

EASTERTIDE

The power to work miracles

I wish you a blessed Easter season. May the risen Christ strengthen you in faithfulness to your Christian calling. This involves sharing not only in the suffering, death and resurrection of Jesus but also in His power to work miracles. It was not without reason that the Lord backed up His words with signs and wonders. He performed His greatest miracle, however, in rising from the dead and going before us to our heavenly home.

According to the truth revealed by Christ, we too shall share in the resurrection to eternal life, as long as we live and die by faith in this truth. Without this faith, without a hunger for God, without a sincere longing to abandon ourselves completely to Him and to expect all things from Him, we can neither follow Christ nor proclaim His Gospel with conviction. Then, too, the signs and wonders will fail to appear which must come to pass in all ages through the name of Jesus.

EASTERTIDE

Five loaves and two fishes

The Gospel tells us how Jesus was followed by a great crowd. They did not yet know what it was that attracted them to Him, but they had heard about Him and they sought Him. What was the meaning of their present life? They were poor from every point of view, and what is more they were hungry.

The disciples of the man of Nazareth had already begun to understand what He signified in their lives, but none of them knew what to do in a situation like this. Master, they said, send this crowd away, because night is falling and they have nothing to eat. Nothing? He said. Do they have absolutely nothing? Go and make sure. And in fact, a few minutes later, the disciples came back with five loaves and two fishes, but what good would they be for such a large crowd? There are certainly five thousand of them. Don't send them away, was His reply, let them sit down; with these loaves and these fishes I can feed them.

They sat down and He took the small amount of food they had given Him, and He multiplied it until all had been fed. Then the disciples understood the significance of the five loaves and two fishes: Jesus needed them, they had to come from the crowd. He would have preferred there to have been more, but even if there had been fifty loaves and twenty fishes, He would have multiplied them and the miracle would have been just as wonderful. Only the joy would have been greater. Because there would have been seventy people giving, instead of one.

But to whom did the multiplication of the loaves and fishes bring the greatest joy? To the little boy who had given five loaves and two fishes and who saw how five thousand were fed.

MAY

Mary

In the divine economy of salvation, Mary has a pre-eminent position. The redemption of mankind began in her virgin womb and, in accordance with the will of God, is only carried to completion with her co-operation and at her intercession. The honour the Church pours on her has its grounds in this sublime calling.

Mary is the mother of the Son of God. She is the most beloved daughter of the Father. She is the spouse of the Holy Spirit. Because of her co-operation in our Lord's work of redemption she is raised high above angels and men. She is worthy of all praise because she is full of grace and because her holiness — already full at her immaculate conception — proved itself for a whole lifetime in her perfect obedience to the will of the Father, even to the bitter end when she became the Mother of Sorrows. There is no one else like her in the Church, whose most pre-eminent member, most shining example and loving mother she is. Even after her assumption into heaven she, the great intercessor, remains intimately linked to all who have recourse to her. Her glory ennobles the whole of mankind. God, who did great things to her, loved her for His own sake and for our sake too; He gave her to Himself and to us.

She is our Mother, our Queen, our example, our helper, our great leader in the fight against the Dragon, the Mediatrix of all the graces we need, and she is worthy of all praise, because out of her has risen the Sun of Righteousness, Christ our God.

MAY

Mary's role in God's plan

Miracles still happen. Maybe it is due only to the rosary of the humble in heart and to their exercise of penance that young people are turning away from Marxism. The prideful opposition to the role allotted to Mary in God's plan we can only break by humbly begging for her help. This is neither behind the times nor against true ecclesiastical renewal.

A gigantic struggle is taking place; it is the struggle between angels and devils for the salvation or destruction of mankind. The leader of the hellish spirits is Satan. At the head of the celestial host stands the Queen of the Angels, whose standard-bearer is St Michael. He who has said 'no' to God has entered the lists against the One who said 'yes'. That is the true sense of the events of the present times.

Because we Christians should know this better than all others, we are more responsible than the others for the present state of world affairs. The world will not change as long as we remain the same. The world is under God's judgement and only penance can help.

THE ASCENSION

A living Gospel

In order to move us to love, God first loved us[47] and showed us His love in the life and death of Christ. And although the Lord is risen from the grave to return to His Father, He nevertheless wishes to remain on earth in a new humanity — our humanity — in order to multiply His love, to draw all men to Himself and to pass through this world in a million different shapes and forms. Through our eyes He wants to smile at men today. With our hands He wants to bind their wounds. With our feet He wants to go after His lost children. With our voices He wants to comfort the sorrowing, teach the ignorant, and denounce in anger the priests and scribes who deceive the people. In our lives He wants to give new proof of His boundless love for God and men.

We bear a heavy responsibility. The Kingdom of Christ on earth depends largely on our witness. Modern man will not be convinced by a Gospel printed on paper, but only by our proclaiming the Good News in living deeds of love. No threat of war, no energy crisis or economic decline can exempt us from this duty.

---

[47] 1 Jn 4:19

AFTER THE ASCENSION

The Master's last command

Since His ascension into heaven our Lord reigns in the glory of God, not only as the Incarnate Son, who for love of His Father allowed Himself to be crucified, but also as the head of His Body, the Church. United with Him through faith and the Sacraments, our life, too, is now 'hidden with Christ in God'[48] and taken up into the life of the triune God. Therefore we must 'look for the things that are in heaven, where Christ is seated at the right hand of God', and fix our thoughts 'on heavenly things, not on things of the earth.' For 'our homeland is in heaven'.[49] The homeland and heavenly dwelling that we must long for is no other than the glorified body of Christ, who will transfigure our wretched bodies to make them like His own.[50]

The apostles, who witnessed their divine Master's ascension, were left behind in a Roman Empire which was perishing because of its immorality. The Lord of time and eternity, for whom empires and civilisations are less than a grain of sand, saw no obstacle in this. He promised His disciples the power of the Holy Spirit and commanded them to spread His teachings to the ends of the earth.[51] 'And they, going out, preached everywhere, the Lord working with them and confirming the word by the signs that accompanied it.'[52]

Never was the Church in such need as after our Lord's ascension and in the persecutions of the first centuries. And never has it carried out its task of evangelising the whole

---
[48] Col. 3:3
[49] Phil 3:20
[50] Phil 3:21
[51] Acts 1:8
[52] Mk 16:20

world as then, in the decadent Roman Empire, when its confessors had to pick their way through the mire of moral decay and the blood and tears of martyred Christians. That should be a comfort to us. It proves that need, sorrow, suffering, restricted liberty, persecution, hunger, poverty, sickness, death and all other trials do not necessarily hinder our eternal happiness but even further it, if we accept them after the pattern of Christ. For Christ did not redeem the world by economic systems or recipes for prosperity, but by His Passion and Cross.

We must make greater sacrifices to carry out the last command our Lord gave us: 'Go, therefore, make disciples of all the nations; baptise them in the name of the Father and of the Son and of the Holy Spirit, and teach them to observe all the commands I gave you.'[53]

---

[53] Mt 28:19-20

PENTECOST

'Woe to me, if I do not preach the Gospel!'

St Paul wrote: 'Woe to me if I do not proclaim the Gospel!'[54] The word 'gospel' means 'good news'. A short summary of this news is: love of God and love of our neighbour. That is the message the Lord proclaimed by His life and death. Woe to me, wrote Paul, if I do not preach this message. And woe to us if we are not good news for one another and a well-pleasing sight for God in prayer and sacrifice, through love, goodness and mercy, in word and deed, like the Samaritan, like Veronica or Simon of Cyrene. Woe to us if we do not proclaim the Gospel.

The Gospel has been printed millions of times on paper. It is sold in all languages. But men today, deceived and despairing, do not ask for a paper gospel. They demand a living Gospel. They hunger for Christ, who is the living Good News. They are waiting for men in whom Christ becomes visible again, in whom they can recognise and love Christ. They demand of us that we should give Christ a living form again.

---

[54] 1 Cor. 9:16

AFTER PENTECOST

Suffering for Christ's sake

We are living in the period after Pentecost. The period in which the young Church, in the strength of the Holy Spirit, faced up to a hostile world. She shared her master's fate. Her children came in conflict with the Powers of Darkness; they were dragged before the courts, imprisoned in dungeons and thrown to the lions. 'But they rejoiced to suffer humiliation for His name's sake.'[55]

It is not easy to rejoice in suffering for Christ's sake. It is true that the Cross loses its weight when we surrender to the will of God, and that our love of Christ gives us the strength to bear crosses that seem unbearable. Undoubtedly God still chooses the weak to confound the strong.[56] But as with the first Christians, who comforted one another, today too God has provided human help for our suffering brothers.

---
[55] Acts 5:41
[56] 1 Cor 1:27

CORPUS CHRISTI

Christ hidden in the Poor

In Holy Communion we receive Christ under the form of bread. In the poor that we meet we receive Him in the form of flesh and blood. It is the same Christ. At the Last Judgement He will say: 'I was hungry, naked and sick, I was homeless and in prison....'[57] He will not know us if we have not known Him in the underfed and the unclothed, in the sick, the refugees, the homeless, the persecuted and prisoners. They are waiting for our love. In them waits Christ.

---

[57] Mt 25:35-45

JUNE

The Triumph of St Norbert

I am writing on the feast-day of our holy father St Norbert. He was a penitent, a shepherd of souls, a reformer of the clergy, a defender of the Pope, an apostle of the Eucharist and a great devotee of the Blessed Virgin. He possessed the virtues and qualities the Church needs in times of decadence. To honour him and encourage you I will tell you how he vanquished heresy.

A certain heretic named Tanchelm undermined the authority of the Pope and the bishops, falsified the concept of the Church, denied the sacrificial character of the Mass, the divinity of Christ and His real presence in the Blessed Sacrament, and led vast numbers of priests to apostasy. As there were no mass-media in those days he terrorised the people with his following of three thousand fanatical followers. For years he controlled Antwerp, but also turned up at Bruges, Louvain, Utrecht, Cologne and even in Rome. Wherever he went he left behind confusion and moral chaos. Princes and bishops dared not oppose him. Countless numbers found in his teaching an excuse for their own weakness and followed him blindly. Others kept silence for fear. In the year 1115 he was murdered at Antwerp.

In the same year Norbert was converted from the rakish life he had led up to the age of 35. He founded our Order at Premontré and by the power of his apostolic preaching he renewed the Church in Northern France, Brabant and Westphalia. In 1123 he was called to Antwerp to rebuild the spiritual ruins left behind by Tanchelm. The situation seemed hopeless. Holy Mass was no longer celebrated. Stolen consecrated hosts lay forgotten in boxes and chests. The last remaining priest in the town was living in incest. The most abominable sins had become acceptable.

Norbert was no thunderer of the wrath of God. He addressed the Lord's erring flock with fatherly kindness: 'Do not be afraid, brothers. I know that it was ignorance and not evil intent that led you to follow lies, which you thought were the truth. If the truth had been preached to you, I am sure you would have accepted it. You let yourselves be led astray easily; even more easily, I hope, you will let yourselves be saved.' He avoided reproaches and words that could wound. He was led only by love that seeks good, believes all things and hopes all things. He wasted no time with dialogues that only appeal to the reason, but sought access to souls by the much shorter way of grace, persuasion and touching hearts. He spoke on God's authority and confirmed the truth of his mission by his holiness of life.

The people of Antwerp threw off the chains of sin and won back the freedom of the children of God. They returned to confession. They brought back the desecrated hosts. Soon the town was transformed. That was St Norbert's Triumph.

Norbert is portrayed holding up the Blessed Sacrament for the adoration of the faithful. Under his feet grovels the heretic Tanchelm, whom he vanquished. His life's work is more up-to-date than ever, as there is no lack of modern Tanchelms. Let us pray that I and all his sons may humbly return to him to continue the work he began at Antwerp.

THE SACRED HEART

*Love of our neighbour exists
in and through the love of God*

I thank God for the love He has poured into your hearts. For this love I have been fighting all my life in a divided world. Again and again I have repeated the words of St John: 'If a man who was rich enough in the world's goods saw that one of his brothers was in need, but closed his heart to him, how could the love of God be living in him?'[58]

This does not mean that we only meet God in our neighbours, in whom Christ is hidden, and even less that we need not give a direct answer to Christ's command: 'You shall love the Lord your God with all your heart, with all your soul, with all your mind and with all your strength.'[59] Faith, acceptance of divine grace, adoration, glorifying God and fulfilling His will are not out of date! Love of God, which is our answer to God's revealing Himself in Christ, must never be supplanted by love of our neighbour. For inhuman as it is to forget the second commandment and limit our love exclusively to God, it is even worse to declare that God is dead, to abolish love of Him, to love only our fellow-men and to treat them like God. That is not love of our neighbour, it is idolatry.

Love of our neighbour can only exist in and through the love of God. It has its roots in the words: 'What you did to one of the least of my brothers you did to me.'[60] It derives its strength from the fact that the Son of God, who is infinitely lovable, identifies Himself with the least of His brothers. They share in His lovableness and have a right to

---
[58] I Jn 3:17
[59] Deut 6:5?
[60] Mt 25:40

the love we owe Him. Anyone who considers the love of God superfluous destroys the reason for which we should love our neighbour. Such a person reduces love, with all its dimensions of holiness, to a mere humanitarian gesture of which even the heathens are capable.

The love that went out from God and was made manifest in Christ and which is given to us as a gift of God, is more than human solidarity. Without it even the noblest human action remains but 'a gong booming and a cymbal clashing.'[61] Without it the most advanced worldly reform and the most radical redistribution of earthly goods are worthless. For 'if I give all that I possess to the poor' (and that would be a great act of human solidarity) '... but am without love, it will do me no good whatever.'[62] I therefore pray that you will be given strength to love God above all things, and your neighbour as yourself.

---

[61] 1 Cor 13:1
[62] 1 Cor 13:3

THE SACRED HEART

The Law of Love

Love demands a personal commitment on behalf of the hungry, the thirsty, the strangers, the naked, the sick, the prisoners and all the others spoken of by Christ in His description of the Last Judgement and in whom He Himself lies hidden. It demands that we recognise and comfort Christ in the least of His brothers and that our enemies are not excluded from this. For love of one's enemies is an essential part of Christianity.

It is our duty to proclaim the law of Christian love without any falsification or watering-down; never to adapt the demands of Christ to suit human weakness; to train those we would win over to grow in the strength of Christ who demands of us that we be perfect as our Father in heaven is perfect.[63] He grants His sunshine and His rain, His grace and His love to good and bad, friend and foe alike.[64]

The friends of God have become more and more numerous. They are all those who, for Christ's sake, suffer persecution or have to leave their homelands. But they are all those, too, who through injustice, exploitation and poverty, through a shortage of priests, or spiritual isolation, are in danger of losing their faith. We can hardly ever go too far in our solidarity with these friends in their need. Following the example of Christ, who gave His life for His friends, we must be prepared to make the greatest sacrifices.

The enemies of God that we must love especially are those who persecute or betray the Church. Love towards these enemies demands that we pray for them without ceasing, in

[63] Mt 5:48
[64] Mt 5:45

the sure hope that they will be converted. Every bastion and stronghold of persecution and perversion of the faith must be besieged by legions of humble souls who concentrate their prayers and their sacrifices on the tyrants and false prophets who are trying to destroy the Kingdom of God.

Christ continues and completes His Passion in all who have to tread their hard Way of the Cross as refugees, in all who are persecuted, oppressed, or who suffer spiritual isolation. As once Veronica and Simon of Cyrene comforted and helped Him on the way to Calvary, so we are now called upon to help Him in the poorest of His brothers, with whom He so explicitly identified Himself.[65] It follows that we must revere the poor as we do Him. Their gratitude is the gratitude of Christ and the only guarantee of His blessing upon the work that we perform in His service.

---

[65] Mt 25:45

JULY

God loves little children

God is the friend of little ones. The emotion that seizes us when we discover in their eyes a glimpse of Paradise lost is only a feeble reflection of what must move the Lord when He sees the purity of His own being mirrored in their untainted souls. They are as fresh as spring flowers and as pure as the morning dew. In them is His delight. That is why He will not have people prevent children, to whom the Kingdom of Heaven belongs, from coming to Him.[66] And the strongest expression of the Master's tenderness handed down to us regards the unknown child that 'He took in His arms.'[67] He loved it so deeply that He identified Himself with it in the amazing assurance that 'whoever receives one such child in my name receives me.'[68] So He demands that we should show children the same respect, care and love that we owe Him. And foreseeing what would happen to His little ones at the hands of unscrupulous corruptors, He flung into the world these terrifying words: 'And if anyone should cause one of these little ones to sin, it would be better for him to have a millstone hung round his neck and to be thrown into the sea.'[69]

---

[66] Lk 18:16
[67] Mk 9:36
[68] Mt 18:5
[69] Mk 9:42

JULY

The suffering of the martyrs is for the good of all

Our persecuted brethren are the élite of God's Church, and it is a task of honour to be one with them. For in Christ's Mystical Body we form a spiritual unity with them which is deeper and firmer than any natural union. If one member suffers, all the rest suffer too.[70] The suffering of martyrs is for the good of everyone. Therefore it is a high privilege to be allowed to suffer contumely for Jesus' sake,[71] to be united to the suffering Christ and to have a part in His work of Redemption. After Christ it is undoubtedly due to the persecuted Christians that the Church, even in these dark times, is *Holy* Church, the Bride of Christ in whom, despite the treachery of so many of her children, God is well pleased.

The first Christians were filled with respect for their brethren who suffered persecution for Christ's sake. The martyrs were the very first to be honoured as saints. The Eucharist was celebrated on their graves to express and strengthen our spiritual union with the sacrifice of their lives.

---

[70] 1 Cor 12:26
[71] Acts 7:41

AUGUST

Christ will not belong to the past

Christ refuses to belong to the past. He wants to be more than a vague figure read of in two-thousand-year-old parables. He wants to be our contemporary. He wants to live on in His Church. What He did long ago in His own human shape, He wants to repeat until the end of time in all those who bear His name and who feed on His most sacred Body and Blood. He wants to break through the framework of His historical existence and go out again and again to look for His lost sheep for love of His Father.

That is why the Lord requires of you and me to give Him a living shape, so that He may once more go forth throughout the world as the good Samaritan, as the father of the Prodigal Son, as the friend of publicans and sinners, as the Good Shepherd and as the protector of the persecuted.

AUGUST

Bringing back the flock

Daily in the monastery churches, monks and nuns come before the Almighty not with festive, smouldering bowls of incense, but with hands full of guilt — like dismayed children who hold out the broken pieces of a vase. They represent the weeping Church. They wrestle with God for the salvation of His lost flock. For it is no longer just one lamb which has to be brought back. Committed Christians are now only a tiny minority. In many people, the love by which God recognises His sheep has died. Where it has died, God has lost His flock.

This should cause us grave concern, but should not discourage us. In the sacred liturgy God's serene voice proclaims in every church: 'Look, I myself will take care of my flock and look after it. As a shepherd looks after his flock when he is with his scattered sheep, so shall I look after my sheep.'[72]

It is heartening to know that God never accepts the loss of those who are to be His for all eternity. Although no one has seen Him and He dwells in inaccessible light,[73] He does not hesitate to leave his place and take upon Himself the painstaking search for His lost sheep. He is the unfathomable being who leaves His heavenly splendour to run calling after His straying lambs. He caused Gospels to be written full of parables proclaiming His concern for all poor and lost creatures. Christ breaks through the limits of His earthly being, in order to bring His lost flock home. Therefore He requires us to lend Him a living form, so that once again He can go through the world as the compassionate Samaritan, as the Good Shepherd, as the defender of the oppressed and as the proclaimer of the Good News.

---
[72] Ezech 34:11-12
[73] Eucharistic Prayer IV

THE TRANSFIGURATION

Reliving the life of Jesus

To continue the life of Jesus is the duty of all Christians, a duty that results from our having been chosen to share the divine life of the only-begotten Son, who lives and reigns for ever in unity with the Father and the Holy Spirit. Until the unknown hour when He will unite us to Himself for eternity, He asks us to follow Him on earth and to relive His life. That means that we must live, think, speak, act, pray, love, suffer and die like Him. For 'whoever claims to be living in Him, must live as Christ lived.'[74] This means that all our deeds must be such that He can accept them as His own. It means that like Him we must belong irrevocably to God, we must be the Kingdom of God, in which His Father is the absolute Lord.

Let us counter hate with love, fear with trust in God, injustice, hunger and suffering with the goodness of the Samaritan, egoism with boundless self-sacrifice, and a life in the spirit of this world with the radiant life of Jesus Christ. Let us strive ever harder to imitate the life of Jesus. Then the Father will recognise in us His only-begotten Son. He will refuse us nothing. He will call us, as on Mount Tabor, 'Beloved child, in whom I am well pleased.'[75]

---

[74] 1 Jn 2:6
[75] Mt 17:5

SEPTEMBER

All men are called to be holy

All men are created in the image of God and are called to become holy, as our Father in heaven is holy. This vocation is hampered by the Prince of Darkness, who with lies and deceit destroys the countenance of God in men, kills the divine life in their souls and makes them blind to Christ, who is the way, the truth, and the life.

The devil works with great cunning. Seldom does he show his true face; he mostly enters the scene as an accomplished actor, disguised as an angel of truth, who is able to deceive even the elect. Peter, speaking from bitter experience, therefore warns us to be vigilant.[76] For those who are not vigilant fall under Satan's spell.

The Church begins her night office with the description of the fight between God and the powers of darkness: 'Why do the heathens rage and the nations forge vain plans? God laughs at them and derides them. Then He commands them in His anger!'[77] The victor is at all events Christ, who will finally break His enemies with an iron rod and smash them like vessels of clay.[78] For He alone is our salvation. He alone is our true life.

---

[76] 1 Pet 5:8
[77] Ps 2:1, 4-5
[78] Ps 2:9

SEPTEMBER

Trusting in God's providence

Not only man but God too is much better than we think. We can hardly ever go too far in trusting to His providence. From years of experience, I know that all the wonderful things that Christ has taught us about the goodness and faithfulness of our Heavenly Father are literally true. God has never put me to shame for having placed my trust in Him. Again and again, He has helped me to fulfil the promises, which have often been rash from a human point of view, that I have made for His sake.

This should not surprise us. It is perfectly natural. For the same God who plants in our hearts the desire to help the Church in need supplements with His almighty grace all that is lacking in us weak humans and awakens in the hearts of the benefactors the love needed to alleviate that need. It is not what we *can* do but rather what we *should* do that must be decisive. For we can do all things in the power of Him who strengthens us.

OCTOBER

Our Lady of Fatima

The revelation of Fatima, which was only a contemporary repetition of purely Gospel truths, teaches us that the root of all evil lies not in political, economic or social abuses but in our own hearts. Therefore a spiritual rebirth is the ineluctable condition for every social and political improvement.

Fatima is inextricably linked with the Communist world revolution, which, to the depths of its being, is a total rebellion against God. At Fatima, Mary revealed the remedy. Her message was given little credence. Consequently the Second World War broke out. It ended with a victory for Communism, which subdued a third of humanity. The consequences were millions of refugees, an Iron Curtain and an unprecedented persecution of Christians.

At Fatima, Mary warned us that whole nations would be destroyed unless we were converted. We do not know which nations are thus threatened with destruction. We do not know whether the great catastrophe can still be averted. We do not know whether we will be among those who survive. But we do know that Mary can crush the head of the serpent.[79] Our Lady of Fatima has shown us the way that leads to victory and to the liberation of the persecuted Church. She did not speak of conformity to this world but of conversion, penance and the recitation of the rosary. Do not reject her message.

---

[79] Gen 3:15

OCTOBER

God is King of all the earth

Time and time again, men of violence have risen up, like Goliath of old, and have challenged the People of God. The Israelites were paralysed with fear. But David knew: 'The Lord will deliver me from the hand of the Philistine.'[80] How often has the Church seen Goliath advancing upon her with sword and armour and overwhelming supremacy! Today too there is no shortage of tyrants, filled with proud confidence in their armoured divisions and atomic weapons. Today too those who challenge God fill us with terror. But God is King of all nations. He created them and scattered them across the face of the earth.

Has anyone ever challenged God in the manner of a Goliath as Hitler did? How impressive it was to see him drawing up his plans, high up in his 'Eagle's Nest' with a view of the Alpine scenery as wide and as splendid as that shown by Satan to Christ from the top of a great mountain. Did the Devil stand beside him there and whisper: 'All of this I will give you if you will fall down and worship me'?[81] But the visitor, wandering among the ruins of the Thousand-Year Reich a few years later, would wonder what had gone wrong with Hitler's plans. And the only answer he would find would be that of the *Magnificat*: 'He has shown might in His arm; He has scattered the proud in the conceit of their hearts; He has put down the mighty from their thrones and exalted the humble.'[82] How often mankind has experienced this! Therefore we must not be discouraged by any danger, any threat of war,[83] any onslaught against God's Kingdom on earth.

---

[80] 1 Sam 17:37
[81] Mt 4:9
[82] Lk 1:51-2
[83] Mt 24:6

Once the immeasurable might of the Roman Empire confronted the young Church. Blood flowed in streams. Murderers, henchmen and traitors were at work among the tiny flock. But it grew in spite of all tribulation. And all that remains of Imperial Rome is ruins. Since then the powers of darkness have joined forces against the Church time and time again. But she is invincible.

HARVEST FESTIVAL

'Give us this day our daily bread'

How many years is it since we prayed for bread in the ordinary sense of the world? Ordinary dry bread. The bread of the poor that Jesus multiplied for the hungry crowd. Bread: not a symbolic expression for everything we need or would like. Just bread.

It looks as though in our case the prayer 'Give us this day our daily bread' has been answered in advance. Unfortunately this is not so. Of every three people on earth, two are suffering from hunger. Therefore each one of us should leave his privileged position and take his place behind the other two who have no bread. The Lord's prayer is the same: 'Give us this day our daily bread.' The three of us: the one who has enough to eat, and the two who are hungry. Not tomorrow or even next week but today, now! For this is the day of hunger... 'and forgive us our trespasses', the prayer continues in the same breath, without even beginning a new sentence. Asking for bread and asking for forgiveness go together, just as our own sins and the hunger of others go together.

ALL SAINTS

The theological virtue of Hope

Every year, every day, every hour brings us nearer to death and, as we hope, nearer to heaven. The theological virtue of Hope is therefore indispensable for every pilgrim on the way to his heavenly home. This hope — the certain expectation of eternal blessedness — does not rest on human promises but on the promises of the infinitely faithful and almighty God. It must not be confused with the hope of an earthly future, bringing a little more health, money or prosperity. It is the opposite. For according to the word of Christ we must lose our lives if we wish to save them.[84]

---

[84] Mt 10:39

ALL SOULS

Heaven, the goal of our life

Reflect on the goal of your life, heaven, and bear in mind that no atheist is able to destroy heaven. Never forget that the Church Militant on earth is inseparably bound with the Church Suffering and the Church Triumphant. Think of God's infinite mercy. Think of the Mother who is still the Mother of all, however lost and astray they may be, and whose sky-blue robe is so ample that every fearful soul on earth can find a soft and protecting fold in it. And consider that the world, which was always a vale of tears, can so easily be transformed into a peaceful garden if only we do not try to build this garden outside our hearts and outside the hearts of those we love, and if only we endure in the belief that peace of heart exceeds all other happiness.

NOVEMBER

Love covers a multitude of sins

I daily celebrate Holy Mass for your intentions, for your struggles and difficulties, for your material and spiritual needs, for the secret sorrow in your life and for the Cross that each one of you has to carry. May God be merciful to you, wipe out your guilt and give you an everlasting reward in heaven. And when on the Last Day He draws up the balance of your life, may He remember that your love covers a multitude of sins[85] and that He can forgive you much because you have loved much.[86]

For love is the greatest commandment. Even though owing to the consequences of Original Sin, natural disposition or external circumstances, you may be weak and defenceless in the onslaught of temptations... as long as you can say with a fallen Peter that you really love Jesus and will do everything you possibly can to help Him when, poor, hungry, naked or persecuted, He comes to you... as long as you can say this, you may confidently appeal to his word: 'Blessed are the merciful, for they will obtain mercy.'[87]

---

[85] Prov 10:12
[86] Lk 7:47
[87] Mt 5:7

NOVEMBER

God's hand caresses the earth

One evening, I seemed to see God working in silence; His Hand moving over the world and touching the deepest roots of matter and of souls. A great Hand creating and healing the earth, gentle as the caressing hand of a mother. Was this the same Hand that with one grasp wrenched a thousand solar systems from the abyss of nothingness? Was it the Hand that had hurled galaxies into space and had kneaded massive rocks like soft wax into shapes of wild beauty? It was indeed the same Hand — just as mighty and grand, but now as careful as the hand of a nurse at a sickbed.

God is not to be understood. He Himself shakes up the pillows of sick humanity. Gently He feels the sore places and supports the broken limbs. For He can hate nothing of what He has made and He cannot despise any of the works of His Hand. That is why He is always re-creating and rejuvenating the breaking earth in the silence of His eternal evening, while mankind sleeps and only the silent stars are witnesses of His love.

God's Hand caresses the earth. His gentle countenance is bent with care over its wounds. The eternal Bearer and Restorer of things walks through His desecrated paradise to draw good from human evil. If that were not possible, He would certainly not permit it; He would block for us the paths of wickedness. For who can prevail against Him? Even the devil stands as a humble servant before His face and faithfully performs the part assigned to him in the drama of creation which is being acted only for the glorification of God.

God did not create evil, for He is love and on the evening of each day of creation He saw that everything was good. He certainly did not want evil, nor did He prevent it, not wishing to destroy the supreme benefit of human freedom, and because even sin is serviceable in His almighty Hand. He is more ingenious than we are. Every time we shatter what He has made, the pieces fall together again in a still finer mosaic in which His wisdom shines brighter than before. He allows evil to exist, but He wanders through the nights of earth as a benefactor to turn it into good.

Serenely and gravely, like a child playing at the riverside, He allows streams of sorrow to flow through the hollow of His Hand until they become tears of remorse and repentance. The tyrants of mankind He turns with the merest touch into tools of eternal salvation. He selects them as carpenters of the world-wide cross of redemption on which His Son will hang and bleed until the end of time to draw us all to Him. He blesses unfruitful hate and the diabolic, annihilating wrath of tyrants and church-persecutors, and behold, they bring forth good fruit: joyful surrender and the gentle patience of the lambs that are permitted to follow the Lamb from eternity. Groaning human wrecks He signs with His grace, making them fellow-sufferers with His Son on Golgotha. Thus afflicted humanity will carry the laurel wreath of the Man of Sorrows to the glorious parade of the Day of Judgement.

God goes even further — He crowns the victims of mad violence and ill-used power as martyrs and saints. His glance falls on all lonely and misunderstood people, on the downtrodden and outcasts of this earth, on the nameless bearers of the heavy universal cross who fall beneath it seven times a day and oftener. He blesses their struggle and their defeat and watches their falling so low into the abyss of abasement with a smile at their childish terror, knowing well that they will be raised again to the skies. The last will become the first, the starving He will satisfy with spiritual food and each lost life He will convert into eternal gain. And to all the grains of corn that have fallen and died in the dark earth He will give the growth and fruitfulness of His divine love.

God renews the face of the earth. He stands as a physician at humanity's bed of suffering. The misshapen work of unknowing creatures He covers with glory. Where His shining fingers lovingly caress, creation lies softly glowing. Astonished as a little boy, that evening I understood something of the mystery of evil. My Bible lay open at the text: 'Behold, I make all things new....' And when God approached from the far depths of His starry sky and filled my cell with His presence, I was not afraid, knowing myself and all others borne up and safe in the palm of His Hand.

DECEMBER

He must increase, but I must decrease

The ecclesiastical year ends with a vision of destruction that opens our hearts to the expectation of Advent and clears our sight in readiness for Him who is to return again. For in the night rises the young day, in the end is the new beginning and in death, life.

The Son of Man who promised to shorten the days of tribulation for the sake of the elect is still ready to save His own. That is why He wishes His Bride, Holy Church, to renew herself continually. She must purify herself from the dust of ages so as to be abreast of her times. She must free herself of formalism and pride. She must abandon abuse of power and force of conscience. She must strip herself of riches. And seeing that we ourselves are the Church, it is our duty to carry out this renewal.

This task is sometimes wrongly understood. In the whole of Church history not a single Council has ever had the intention to adapt Christian life to the spirit of the world. All true reforms aimed at a return to the spirit of Christ. John the Baptist expressed the mark of their truth by saying: 'He must increase, but I must decrease.'[88] If God is belittled and man is exalted, there is no question of renewal but of decay. The 'adulthood' of God's people then becomes questionable in the light of Christ's word: 'I thank thee, O Father, because thou hast hidden these things from the wise and the prudent and hast revealed them unto babes.'[89]

These 'babes' are the same as the 'poor in spirit' whom the Lord called blessed. Their poverty is not an economic

---
[88] Jn 3:30
[89] Mt 11:25

phenomenon but a grace. They are not necessarily poor in money but poor in the spirit of the world. They have withdrawn into the inner kingdom of God's presence. They are free from earthly things and ready for anything for the Kingdom of God. The riches of the soul is their share. In spite of their smallness they are inwardly great. They consider earthly happenings from the highest standpoint, for God has revealed to them what He has withheld from the proud and they know exactly what is of importance. They are the silent watchers with a universal viewpoint. By their clear, spiritual decisions they take care that their light is not extinguished in the darkness of these times. They are a tiny flock. They are easily overlooked. Their silent service in prayer and penance is as nothing compared to the noisy activity in Church and world. But God is not in thunder, He is in silence.[90]

---

[90] Cf. 1 Kg 19:11-12

DECEMBER

Without God, nothing can change

Louder than ever the Church calls in our times: 'Come, Lord, and deliver us, do not delay!'[91] In this cry of distress she lends her voice to all who crave deliverance. Those who have experienced war and occupation know what it is to be liberated: the day independence is regained, the day the hated uniforms disappear, but also the day of reckoning, of unchained passions, burning houses, manhandled women and cowardly judges. Not infrequently an intoxication that in the pale light of re-awakening proves to be a lie.

Without God nothing can change, for no outward liberation can free men from themselves, nor can it reform them spiritually, make them different and better. If a man has been spoiled and falsified there is only One who can restore him to his original soundness: the Creator who made him. He can change a man inwardly: can re-create him and renovate him.

Christ did this two thousand years ago. He liberated man from his sins and his enmity with God; He reconciled him with the Heavenly Father and made him His child. This liberation, although it did not undo the outward terror set in motion by Herod, was no lie but an inward reality, it made all men children of one Father, brothers and sisters of each other, and so restored peace on earth. The first Christmas grace was this: that there was again a man of whom God could say: 'This is my beloved Son, in whom I am well pleased.'[92] This new Man — was the Firstborn[93] of the new People of God, who serve the Father in peace and freedom and so win happiness.

---
[91] Mass of the 24th December, Introductory Prayer
[92] Mt 3:17
[93] Col 1:18

CHRIST THE KING

*With your money you can console,
with your suffering you can redeem*

Christ proclaimed His kingship when He stood before Pilate as a beaten and defeated man. His friends had deserted Him. Judas had betrayed Him. Peter had denied Him. Forsaken by all, He cast His complaint at the unheeding sky: 'My God, why hast Thou forsaken me?'[94] He died as a failure. But in this lay His triumph. He is a King in His defeat.

Christ's life is the standard for each Christian life. In spite of weakness and fear, we are called to relive His life and die His death, and hereafter to share His victory. The work that we are accomplishing also stands under this basic law of Christianity. The Church in need is therefore better helped by our sufferings than by our donations. With your money you can console, but with your suffering you can redeem.

Every suffering Christian bears the cross of Christ as his contribution towards the redemption of the world. Let our hearts too be purified by repentance, penance, prayer, fasting and good works; let them share in the Passion of Our Lord — silent, attentive, helping, sacrificing with Him and dying with Him — in order to rise with Him hereafter.

You too have your sorrow, your cross, your weakness. Do not let them embitter you. Do not ask to understand what God wishes to conceal from you still. Do not doubt His love. Say with a smile that what God does to you is well done.

God is preparing His future. Only what has been purified in suffering can be used by Him tomorrow. God cleanses His tools; He is cleansing His Church.

---
[94] Mk 15:34; Ps 22:1

Prayer to Mary

Mother Mary, we come to you in the raging storm which the Prince of Darkness has unleashed. You see how at least two hundred million of your Catholic, Protestant and Orthodox children send up their sighs, suffering the terror of the enemies of God who wish to tear down the Almighty from His throne and to destroy His Kingdom in the hearts of the faithful. You see how fifteen million refugees have been uprooted and are now in danger of losing all hope. You see how in the Third World countless exploited millions are stranded on the shore of our selfishness. And you see how the smoke of Satan has even seeped through into the Holy of Holies; that the storm of confusion is battering even the most sheltered bay and the safest haven in God's Church. Even the most elect are being torn from their moorings and away from God. You see how priests of every rank and dignity have lost their bearings and are sabotaging the course set by Peter, scuttling his ship in the midst of the foaming waters. And Jesus sleeps.

Mother, if even the Apostles lost their courage in the storm, you will understand our fear. Tell your Son that he must hear our almost desperate prayer: 'Lord, save us, for we perish!'

Yes, Mother, we are afraid in the face of confusion, the division and the unfaithfulness to God, which are now spreading like a plague throughout the Church. Is not the cleft that divides the People of God a collective sin against the Holy Spirit? Do you not see, Mother, that the strivings for unity with our separated brethren and the efforts to preach the old faith in a new way go hand in hand with boundless excesses which are inflicting incalculable harm on the unity, peace, tranquillity of conscience and loyalty to their faith of countless Catholics?

What we are now witnessing is not a crisis of growth, but actual decay; not the springtime with all its promise but the dark autumn; not the bursting forth of new life, but the wholesale fall of dead branches and dry shoots which have lost all contact with the vine that is Christ. Instead of permeating the world with the leaven of the Gospel, the People of God allows itself to be thrown into turmoil by the leaven of the world, even though Christ has unequivocally broken with this world.

Mother, now that the need is at its greatest and the powers of darkness seem to have free rein, we come to you with childlike trust and implore your powerful aid. Now swept away and rudderless on the waves of this age, we place ourselves, together with all disfigured humanity and our work for the Church in need, in your maternal hands.

We consecrate ourselves to you, dear Mother of Fatima. Preserve us in the love of your Son, protect us from the evil of this world and lead us safe to the heart of God. And when we have passed through death's dark gate and stand before the judgement seat of your Son, grant that we may find you there to welcome us with a smile and that we may say without fear: 'Here we are, Mother.'

CONTENTS

First Week in Advent: *God has gone*	5
Second Week in Advent: *The Star of Bethlehem*	7
Third Week in Advent: *The Tragedy of the Christmas story*	8
Fourth Week in Advent: *The peace of Christ*	10
Christmas Eve: *'Tomorrow injustice will be swept away from the earth!'*	12
Christmas Day: *It is Christmas a thousand times a year*	14
Christmas Day: *Christmas without Christ?*	15
The Flight into Egypt: *One particular case*	16
New Year: *New Year's wishes*	17
New Year: *A year has started*	18
January: *Renewing our lives*	19
February: *The hidden life of Jesus*	20
February: *Blessed are the pure in heart*	21
March: *The cycle of the seasons*	22
March: *We are the salt of the earth*	23
Ash Wednesday: *We must not think that we are without guilt*	24
First Week in Lent: *Turn again to the Lord your God*	25
Second Week in Lent: *Man does not live on bread alone*	27
Third Week in Lent: *The Church's task to relieve human need*	29
Fourth Week in Lent: *Rich or poor for eternity*	30
Fifth Week in Lent: *We can judge only ourselves*	32
Passiontide: *We must glory in the Cross of Christ*	33
Holy Week: *A 'sensible' Messiah?*	35
Maundy Thursday: *Christ's priests*	36
Good Friday: *Forsaken Jesus*	37
Holy Saturday: *Pietá*	39
The Easter Vigil: *Alleluia!*	40
Easter Day: *'Why do you seek the living among the dead?'*	41
Eastertide: *The power to work miracles*	43
Eastertide: *Five loaves and two fishes*	44
May: *Mary*	45
May: *Mary's role in God's plan*	46
The Ascension: *A living Gospel*	47
After the Ascension: *The Master's last command*	48
Pentecost: *'Woe to me, if I do not preach the Gospel!'*	50
After Pentecost: *Suffering for Christ's sake*	51
Corpus Christi: *Christ hidden in the Poor*	52
June: *The Triumph of St Norbert*	53
The Sacred Heart: *Love of our neighbour exists in and through the love of God*	55
The Sacred Heart: *The Law of Love*	57
July: *God loves little children*	59
July: *The suffering of the martyrs is for the good of all*	60

August: *Christ will not belong to the past*	61
August: *Bringing back the flock*	62
The Transfiguration: *Reliving the life of Jesus*	63
September: *All men are called to be holy*	64
September: *Trusting in God's providence*	65
October: *Our Lady of Fatima*	66
October: *God is King of all the earth*	67
Harvest Festival: *'Give us this day our daily bread'*	69
All Saints: *The theological virtue of Hope*	70
All Souls: *Heaven, the goal of our life*	71
November: *Love covers a multitude of sins*	72
November: *God's hand caresses the earth*	73
December: *He must increase, but I must decrease*	76
December: *Without God, nothing can change*	78
Christ the King: *With your money you can console, with your suffering you can redeem*	79
Prayer to Mary	80

The Author

Werenfried van Straaten was born in Mijdrecht, Holland, on 17th January 1913. He studied Classics at university; he intended to join the Capuchins, but could not because of ill-health, and in 1934 he entered the Norbertine Abbey of Tongerlo, Belgium. Deeply moved by the plight of the homeless and dispossessed exiles in devastated Germany following the Second World War, he set out single-handed to provide for their spiritual and physical needs. He helped three thousand 'Rucksack Priests' to provide the Sacraments and spiritual help, and converted trucks into mobile chapels to visit those parts of Germany where there were no Catholic churches. He begged for food, money, and clothes. He earned his reputation by begging for bacon, being rewarded with hundreds of tons of bacon — and his nickname, the 'Bacon Priest'.

After his meeting with Cardinal Mindszenty during the Hungarian Uprising in 1956, Fr Werenfried expanded the work of Aid to the Church in Need to help the persecuted Church in Eastern Europe and the refugees from Communist persecution. In 1959 he visited the refugee camps of South Korea, Hong Kong and South Vietnam, which led him to begin to work to support refugees worldwide. In 1962, Pope John XXIII asked Fr Werenfried to extend the activities of the charity to the poor Church in Latin America; in 1965, after visiting Africa and seeing the need there, he extended the work of Aid to the Church in Need there too.

In 1988, at the age of 75, Fr Werenfried retired as head of Aid to the Church in Need, but continued to work in his capacity as founder of the organisation. He describes his work in two books, *They call me the Bacon Priest* (first published 1961) and *Where God Weeps* (1969).

Aid to the Church in Need

Aid to the Church in Need is one of the largest Catholic charities in the world, with 600,000 benefactors in fourteen countries. We support some seven thousand projects every year.

Training Seminarians
We help provide for more than 16,000 future priests who are desperately needed throughout the world. More and more young men are coming forward for the priesthood in Eastern Europe and the Third World, and the dioceses and religious orders need help with the ever-increasing cost of training and formation.

Broadcasting and the Media
Aid to the Church in Need helps broadcast the Word of God on *Radio Blagovest* and *Radio Voskresinnya* to the former Soviet Union and on *Radio Veritas* to Vietnam: for many remote areas of Asia and Latin America the radio is the most important evangeliser. Now we also produce TV programmes and videos to teach the Faith.

The Children's Bible
We have already printed more than 20 million *Children's Bibles* in seventy languages, and are sending out hundreds of thousands of copies every year: in many parts of the world children learn to read and write using this Bible. We are now translating and producing a new colour edition, *God Speaks to His Children*.

Transport for pastoral work
In the beginning the 'Bacon Priest' provided motor-bikes and VW Beetles for priests; and today in the far-flung dioceses, chapel-trucks are rolling again. Help is needed with anything from bicycles for catechists to Land Rovers for priests and nuns.

Supporting priests and religious
Aid to the Church in Need is helping priests and religious to live and minister in the poorest parts of the world. We are supporting sixty-five contemplative communities in Poland. The life and prayer of the Church depends on our help for these priests and sisters.

Building churches
Each year we help with the construction and restoration of churches, seminaries, presbyteries and convents. We are continuing to build bush chapels in Africa and Asia and parish centres in Latin America, and to rebuild churches in Eastern Europe.

Printing books for Eastern Europe
Aid to the Church in Need receives hundreds of letters a day from Eastern Europe, asking for religious literature; and we respond to each individual request. A Ukrainian woman wrote: 'We need the Bible more than our daily bread.'

Helping refugees
Right from the start **Aid to the Church in need** has given aid to refugees. And today — whether in the Middle Wast, Asia, or Africa — we ease the suffering of those who flee persecution and oppression.

Aid to the Church in Need is a Universal Public Association within the Catholic Church, dependent on the Holy See, providing pastoral relief to needy and oppressed Churches and aiding refugees. Registered Charity No. 265582.